# SELF MASTERY

# SELF MASTERY

## TO REACH HIGHER CONSCIOUSNESS

CINDY

# CONTENTS

# CHAPTER 1

# INTRODUCTION

Self-Mastery to higher consciousness is a journey we all as one came to earth to discover. Who we are and why we are here? I am sure it is a quest for all the seekers. I remember when I was young, I was disgusted with poverty while living in the projects. I thought, *is God real? If so, where is he?* I start questioning reality. At the age of twenty-seven, I reached a breaking point from failed relationships, not staying healthy, and unfruitful jobs. As an adult, I stood in my apartment contemplating my suicide! I always had a passion for helping others, but I knew I had to master my life first. I knew as a kid from my gut(intuition) that something great can become of one's life if we only apply ourselves.

Having this inner knowing made me go on a journey of truth! The last seven years of studying my life; I observe the lives of others around me. My observation started after enrolling in the University of Metaphysic in the year 2011. I realize self-mastery is a challenging task. That is why so many people make a conscious choice to stay content where they are in their lives. I discover nothing stopping us in life but ourselves. I felt like a robot doing a routine job of nine to five, coming home to eat, watch Tv, then waking-up to only complete the cycle all over again! I thought, *there must be more to life than this?* My negative belief system since I was young was controlling and dictating my life unconsciously. I learned that ninety percent of our action is control from our subconscious thought. I wondered; *do I have to reprogram my mind?*

It is worth it, even if we must start all over! The first step, I completely stop watching Tv. "For as a man thinketh in his heart, so is he" (Proverbs 23:7). I had a desire to tap into my God-given abilities. I also knew it is God plan for all humanity; if only we would master our thoughts. "For I know the plans that I have for you, declares the Lord. Plans to prosper you and not harm you. Plan to give you hope and a future" (Jeremiah 29:11). It took me seven years to study my life, and I become aware of my healing abilities, visions, and dreams. I thought *we would spend that time anyway investing in a traditional college. Why not invest in ourselves?* I wrote three books. All information and wisdom were downloaded into my mind from my higher self.

My lessons learned was through my writing on *Cosmo Connections*(self-awareness). I learn to change my inner thoughts to match my desirable outcome. "Like attracts like, so when we think a thought, we attract it to us" (Byrne, 25). I learned this great truth from studying the book called, *The Secret*. The secret gives us anything we want from health, love, wealth, and happiness if we master ourselves. I thought, *is this life available to everyone?* "Absolutely!"

Then I became aware that life is not something that happens to us, but for us. In the book called, *Your Essential Self* it stated; "a third of us are life-seekers; a third is death seekers, and the rest is content of remaining asleep" (Ching,111). I wanted to be among the life seekers, so I knew it was vital to keep searching and applying the knowledge to my life. "Ask, and it will be giving to you; seek, and you will find; knock, and the door will be opened to you" (Matthew 7:7).

I notice many people that walk the earth including myself at one point victimized themselves. That was me; having a pitting party! Then I realize birds of a feather flock together. Back then I heard people in my environment complaining, so I start to do the same. Drawing more of unwanted results into my life. In the book of *total forgiveness*, it stated, "True forgiveness destroy the record they might have used to vindicate themselves" (Kendall,143).

If we all want to master our lives and reach higher consciousness; it starts with gratitude. I start being grateful for the current life I have; living in the moment. I develop a love affair with nature. I remember when I was a kid, the park excited me! I wanted that joy back. To do so, I must live in that moment of happiness every day. Suffering and adversity became my greatest insights! I realize there are two polarities of everything. I thought *the opposite of it is my opportunity to turn it around.* It is not what happens to us that dictate the outcome; it is how we handle adversity.

In the book of *Joy*, it spoke about roots to virtue! It is nonattachment, compassion, and wisdom. (Dalai, 147). Another insight that helps me reach consciousness was learning from my dreams. Messages allow me to see my walking of life. I knew flying was a key to me controlling my destiny. Water represents the emotions that were taking over me! However, when I see monsters in my dream, I would often disappear, run, or transcend through the walls. I realize it was time for me to face it! Fear is an illusion, and if I want to master myself, I had to face and own up to my inner demons. I thought, *who are those evil entities? Is it me?* "It sure is!"

My old self was afraid of the new change and wanted to stay comfortable. We all know change hurts and it takes courage to master yourself. Carl Jung stated the reason we dream is to compensate the psyche parts that are underdeveloped in our walking of life. In contrast, Sigmund Fred said it is to preserve sleep; which is contradicting because of REM (rapid eye movement) during the dream. I realize the only way for me to master my life is to get back in touch with the creator. Whether it be God or higher self; we need to tap into this wisdom. In the book of *Understanding the Purpose and Power of a Woman*; "a woman cannot fulfill her purpose unless she is in the relationship with God" (Munroe,99). My philosophy of this great truth is coming back in *oneness* with ourselves!

# CHAPTER 2

# RESILIENCE

Self-mastery is a necessary condition of being free and a better living. It was detected in the universal history in, *Dialectic of Enlighten.* It stated; "the wholly enlightened earth is radiant with triumphant calamity." When it comes to stress and well-being, it plays a role in negative and positive emotions. It is not from a single situation but interacting in the process of meditation on life experience, physical response, and psychological. It is the process of coping and appraisal. Coping involves the reaction to the focus emotion. An appraisal is evaluating whether the person has the resources to cope effectively or deal directly with the stressor. Appraisal also deals with the threat to the well-being and find ways to manage (Tiberio, 311).

Everyday life is strains and hassles, but not all experience could be handling as stress. The current study focuses on environmental mastery, resilience resources, and self-esteem. I remember before I discover who I was I had low self-esteem. I was walking around the earth with no sense of direction. Aimless failing situations because of the direction my mind was taking me. For example, I would accept jobs paying me eleven dollars an hour with a bachelor's degree in that field of study. Now that I think about it, *they got a good deal for their money. But did I?* I love serving humanity, but I knew I had to develop ways to change my life as well. I start to stand in my position as a leader from my inner knowing while living my life on purpose.

"Environment mastery is a form of control regardless of one's ability to bring the intended outcome" (Lachman, 1994). We all learn this through self-exploration Those with high self-esteem can cope with problems and circumstances. They are less likely to become overwhelmed in the face of adversity (Tiberio,311). Resilience resources is when people go through positive or negative changes. It is from a person thought and environment influence. Self-esteem is how the person interprets the stress of their daily life. "People see circumstances individually and global each day. Self- esteem and environmental mastery are expected to moderate the process of stress appraisal" (Montpetit, 314). "Having a positive self-attitude embody psychological impact on one's life" (Pearlin & Schooler, 1988). The research stated that levels of self-esteem do not control a person life, "it is self-esteem stability that contributes to resilience functioning" (Kernis, 2005). Resilience is remaining stable minded during adversity.

Once I realize everything in the process of learning and growing it allows me to see things differently. I was working a part-time job at the time when I came in the house from my morning walks. As I was getting ready to take a shower, the lights would not turn on. I thought *it must be the switch.* I gave the turn off notice bill to my roommate, and he said he would take care of it, our agreement since I have taken care of it for the last eight months. I was in denial. I went downstairs to flick the lights and still not power. I thought, *oh my goodness we have no electricity.*

I admittedly text my roommate and blabbing my mouth about his failure to hold up his obligations. Then I realize, wait a minute as I calm down. In return, he was panicking saying he do not have the total amount for the turn-off notice of five hundred and twenty-four dollars. It was the last minute on his part, but I was responsible for how I respond. As he continues to yell, I kept quiet and realized it was a process of learning. I was even happy he expresses himself because he holds things in and builds up stress. My mind went to work to seek out resources when it remains calm. Within a couple of hours, he was able to pay three hundred while I seek out money to pay the remaining balance. I could only image people that have to deal with this kind of stress more than a couple of hours with no electric or resources. I notice when we challenge aspect of ourselves and find our life purpose and walk towards it, all kinds of things will discourage us and come falling. I am here to tell you remain faithful! Do what you can do in your ability and let the rest go. Surrender! Before that my cell phone turned off for nonpayment. Wow, I thought, *no cell phone?* I sat in my room in peace. I said to myself, *Lord you know where I am, and you have all the resources!* It was a good experience not to have my cell phone on for two days. No social media! Not checking my text! Okay, Lord, I am fine.

As I sat on my bed staring at the ceiling. Was I okay? No, but I did accept what was happening. I was looking forward to my first book to be released soon. I focus on what I did do and not what I did not do. My youngest daughter came rushing through the house in an uproar! "Your cell phone not working?" she said. I smiled and said, no it is not. "What is wrong with you?" "You have grandma and my dad is wondering what is going on." *How many people will panic without technology?* Could we walk away from our cell phone for three hours? I told my daughter I did everything in my power and the rest is in God's hands. I was content because I acted! I email my enrollment counselor to let him know my phone will be off for a couple of days or so. He said, no problem! I'm sure he understood graduate students face problems. Everyone else was wondering what is wrong with her. I was mastering myself. "I discipline my body and bring it into subjection because if I don't when I preach to others, I should be disqualified." (1 Corinthians 9:27)

Within one hour I received resources, and it was paid! When the body is calm resources flow to us easily. We should never have to beg or plead for help. Stay calm! When in doubt and fear, it is not in the order of faith. Therefore, the blessing that was on the way stop dead in its track because we unconsciously rejected it! The battle kept coming, and I know if I deal with it fearlessly it will be over soon. Storms never last!

Sure, enough my roommate came home the next day with an eviction notice from the mailbox. He was panicking with his eyes bulging out of his head. "What?" I said. "Well if you do not see a problem with it, so be it." He replied. He slammed the house door and pulled off in his car. I thought, *Geesh, what's wrong with him?*

At that moment I became self-aware of how I was handling stress. It is not that I didn't see it as a problem. I saw an opportunity to solve a problem. I looked at the calendar and realized we have five days before we are evicted! I stared at the eviction notice, and something did not seem right. He paid his part of the rent leaving me with the remaining balance for April. Then he paid his part of the rent again and left me with the remaining balance for May. I was only doing and working on what I require me to do and left the rest in God's power!

I continue to stare at the notice with awareness. Aha! *Why did they not apply May rent to take care of the remaining balance of April*? The total rent was $1600. He paid $800 for April and $800 for May since we were already in May. I phone the rent office. *"Why wasn't $800 for May applied to April rent?"* She said I am sorry ma'am disregard that notice! Great, now I can catch up on May since the month is not over yet.

I was excited about the solution so; I phone my roommate. "Hey, we are okay and not getting evicted," I told him. He had already hit a depressive state. "You could phone the people if you like," I said. I try to explain the solution to him, but he couldn't apply the information because his mind had already taken over his entire body. He was drained and he said I don't feel like calling anyone. I thought, *why was he not excited about the solution*? We have the power to steer our mind in the direction of victory or defeat. *Which direction will you choose*? I choose victory!

I was aware of the things going on around me. I knew my cell phone was overdue, car insurance, and rent. However, every morning I went for a walk to listen to inspirational videos. How we start our day determine which direction our mind will go. Our dominant thoughts dictate our life! Even though my environment was in chaos my mind saw success. I remain in self-control and continue working on my projects. *Do I always stay positive*? No! When I see the negative vampire within myself trying to creep in, I shift it to something that will serve me for my good. Do not give it any attention because it will suck the life out of you!

If we want to reach consciousness, we must be honest with myself. I cannot walk around thinking I am better than anyone. I have fault and failure I must deal with as it arises. We all are humans and deserve respect. People often look down on others for their flaws. I notice when walking my journey, I must own up to my light and dark side.

I realize it is okay to get upset, sad, and angry. It is my self-awareness. Once I release it, then and only I discover my identity. When I did suppress these energies, it comes out in disorienting ways. I want to take control of it, so I release it respectfully when it arises. Who can say, "I have kept my heart pure? I am clean and without sin?" (Proverbs 20:9)

Humans make mistakes, but it is our job to own up to it and release it. "There is no one who does not sin" (1 Kings 8:46). It does not matter how to enlighten one claims to be; there will always be darkness. If we were glorious, *why are we here on earth to learn?* It is a learning journey to master ourselves daily. I had to leave the traditional church because the messages did not resonate with me (not all churches). Pastor's was speaking a lot about living in the light but not owning our dark energy. "And he closed the book, he gave it back to the minister and sat down. All the eyes of people in the synagogue was fastened on him" (Luke 4:20). If we hide these aspects of ourselves, *how could we bring it to the light?*

# CHAPTER 3

# STOP BLAMING OTHERS

People say they live righteous to do God's work. If that is the case why did Jesus walk, eat, and sat with sinners? People should start shining their light on the truth, then and only we discover ourselves. "There is not a righteous man on earth who does what is right and never sin" (Ecclesiastes 7:20). When I read this verse, I was relieved! My only fear at the time was when I start moving toward the light was my negative self-talk and thinking. It was exposed! "If we claim we are without sin, we deceive ourselves, and the truth is not in us" (1 John 1:8). There were all kinds of feelings coming up. It was jealousy, bittiness, and hate.

When we choose to only walk in darkness(ego) we do not recognize it. This is when we see with the eyes of awareness the understanding of oneself. I had to sit with my entire being to see where it was coming from. I thought, *how would I own up to this and fix it?* We always blame others for our sins. I had to realize it was mine and no one else problem. "The Lord God said to the woman, what have you done?" "The woman said, the serpent tricks me, that is why I ate the fruit" (Genesis 3:13). As I meditate on this verse, God went to each one of them even though he left the man in charge of the garden. Everyone responsible for their actions. Adam said he was afraid when he heard the voice of God. I am sure we all would have been scared. If the scripture was turned the other way around, and they admit their sins, *would it still be the falling of man?*

Instead of blaming others God wants us to admit to our wrong. "Then I confessed my sins. I did not hide my wrongdoing and you forgave all my sins" (Psalm 32:5). I discover before I start pointing out blame and fault on others, I should be self-aware of myself. After my darkness rises, I work on one part of myself at a time. When I mastered it, I moved on to the next discovery. When I start seeing other people faults without working on myself first, I heard a voice, "Why do you look at the speck of sawdust in your brother's eye and do not see the plank in your eye?" (Matthew 7:3)

I realize based on this scripture it was my mirror of self I had to improve. I thought, *is that something within me that needs to be fixed?* My greatest insights into self-awareness was trigger points. Anything that affects me emotionally was what I need to work on within myself. A lot of people do not want to sit with their emotions because it is painful. My challenging part of self-mastery was accepting the vulnerable part of myself. I always thought it was a form of weakness, another false belief. I also gave my ego control back then. To live in the truth and accept what God (universe) have for me, I had to let go! "For he was crucified in weakness but lives by the power of God" (II Corinthians 13:4).

Once and for all, I had to forgive myself. I used to blame myself for the wrong choices, and I felt guilty. It was a sign I did not release it to God even though I confessed it. "If we confess our sins, he is faithful and just and will forgive us, purify us of all unfruitfulness" (1John 1:9). I thought, *why did I not forgive myself?* Having self-worth is vital to master oneself. I had to realize I am important to myself and God. "Your thoughts are of great worth to me, God! If I could number them, there would be more than the sand. When I arise, I am still with you" (Psalm 139:17).

# CHAPTER 4

# SHIFT YOUR ENERGY

The bible warns us about self-control. We either control our life or be a slave to what controls us. We could take self-control over lust, food, money, and our words. Having control over our lives is the foundation of living. We have the power to put sin under control! (1Corinthisans 9:25). God plan for our life is to live fully alive and free.

In the book of *total forgiveness*, it helps us master ourselves. It uses Jesus words of the father forgive them. It not only forgives but releases the person. In similar the book called, *The Secret* in the law of attraction, also in biblical terms; Ask, Believe, and Receive! We cannot help our environment by focusing on negative things. We only add more of the same. Instead one should shift their energy to trust, peace, abundance, and love (Kendall, 71).

Change seems to overtake us when we least expect it. The power of change is unconscious unless we discover who we are and where we are going. "Self-discovery is a personal healing and acknowledgment." (Harvey, 30) After studying my life for seven years and others, I start to see the soul calling. Under every pain is the opposite desire of truth! I notice instead of people complaining about their job; they should find another one or create it.

Not knowing who we are cause a lack of confidence, unworthily, and victim to our circumstance. The opposite polarity is we all are talent, worth, and lovable. "When we hang in there and keep trying, we cross the threshold of transformation" (Harvey, 145).

A dream is an opportunity to examine our life on stage. It reveals our fears, anxiety, and threats to our environment. I recall the vivid dreams I had of soaring, fear, and it was life changing. "He will never leave you nor forsake you. Do not be afraid, do not be discouraged" (Deuteronomy 31:8). *We must decide if we want to live in fear or freedom*? I choose freedom!

# CHAPTER 5

# HOW DO YOU SEE YOURSELF?

There are different beliefs about leadership development. They have character and attitude. They see themselves and the world in a different perspective. Two most encouraging animals in the Bible is the Eagle and Lion. *Why is that?* The lion has courage. *Why is he different?* The way he approaches his environment. He is respected in his kingdom. "A lion sees things he can eat. His mind knows he can eat it! So, because of its thinking, he attaches it!" (Munroe, 2017) If a man does not see himself as a leader, he will go around aimlessly with no sense of direction. "Our thinking allows us to view things differently. It is what we believe about ourselves" (Munroe, 2017). "Now unto him, that is able to do exceedingly abundantly above all that we ask or think, according to the power that worketh in us" (Ephesian 3:20).

If we want to expand our limits, we should change our belief systems. I remember growing up in a poor household my family would say, "money does not grow on trees." I took it as money was hard to get. As I change my belief about money, I start to co-create.

There are unlimited resources in the universe. When we create things and share it with the world, we enter the law of exchange. Our life is what we think it should be. The right attitude steps up for an opportunity. I change my perception of who I am. If we never discover who we are, we will always work under someone else authority. I had to realize I am important to humanity, and the universe, so I went on self-discovery!

Cultivating our attitudes and beliefs shapes our life. When people ask where we come from our response should be source energy. Knowing this truth expanded my territory in my mind. Leaders develop friends base on their destination. We must continue to study the universe and ourselves to discover and understand life. Eagles never flock together. I always thought something was wrong with me because I had one trusted best friend. Most people had a group of friends posted all over social media. I had to learn eagles flies alone, and it's bold. I had to turn away from family and old friend's beliefs to walk my path. What we think is important than what we do. Leaders help train other leaders. They do not need followers; we want other leaders to join us. "On the high mountain of Israel, I will plant it, that it may bring forth fruit. And birds of every kind will nest under it; they will nest in the shade of its branches" (Ezekiel 17:23).

Having a leadership mentality is taking a risk. Sometimes it comes under pressure to walk alone to self-discovery. It is how we respond to our environment. I had to nurture myself with inspirational books, videos every day for eight months. That is when my life shifts from the polarity of negative to positive. Everyone can be a leader; it is fear that holds them back. I discovered I have a couple of gifts. I focused on one at a time.

The way we think about ourselves determine the direction our life will go. I had to change my perception of myself and the way I view the world. Living in poverty when I was young was self-realization for me to discover, *what is life?* Instead of focusing on the outcome as an adult I start asking questions. People would say, *are you a philosopher?* I wanted to know the truth about the world and the people living in it. I used to avoid it, and it causes me to be depressed. Hiding from the truth will not change anything. "Then you will know the truth, and the truth will set you free" (John 8:32).

When I discover this, I found out leaders in the most organization was living a lie. One manager told me she was following the rules to play it safe. I remember in the year 2015 I gained over fifty pounds. I was following everyone else routine at the time. It was blocked energy inside of me. Then I thought, *that's enough!* I could not continue to do this to myself bringing more sickness to my mind and body. "Believe not about yourself based on ignorance of mass-minded people but abide in God from within you" (Masters, 38).

# CHAPTER 6

# RELATIONSHIP USED AS CATALYST

One blessing to self-mastery is relationship used as the catalyst. I used to look at it as me victimizing myself. I never realize it was awareness. I encounter the unsolved issue from childhood and a wrong belief system. I left people in charge of my happiness, but I was the one that could only live up to my standards. I had to love myself and forgive others. I could not expect people to live up to my desires and longings. I remember watching the movie Wizards of Oz, when Dorothy said, "please help me!" "The power is within you!" We all have this source and strength within us. Once we reach self-mastery to higher consciousness, we will never depend on others for our happiness.

After we reach self-mastery, we no longer project hidden aspect of ourselves on others. It is our responsibility to live up to our truth and stop blaming others. Other people are not responsible for our shortcoming and failure. If we are not happy with our employment, it is a key to ourselves that we seek more out of life. Instead of continuing complaining I had to discover, *what do I want to do with my life?* Once I tap into my higher self, my soul was ready to work! It was a hidden part of myself that wanted to be revealed. It was my passion to reach the world through the art of writing. The only way I knew was to get in touch with myself. When my self-confidence builds up, and I knew the power was within me, I was able to deal with problems as it arises. Even though self-mastery to reach a higher consciousness is a continuous process, I had to work on myself daily and never stop learning.

Every day I had to be careful so nothing of the world would come into my mind (false beliefs). "Do not live by the behavior of others. But let God transform your mind, so you will know and learn God's will for your life" (Romans 12:2).

# CHAPTER 7
# TRANSFORMATION

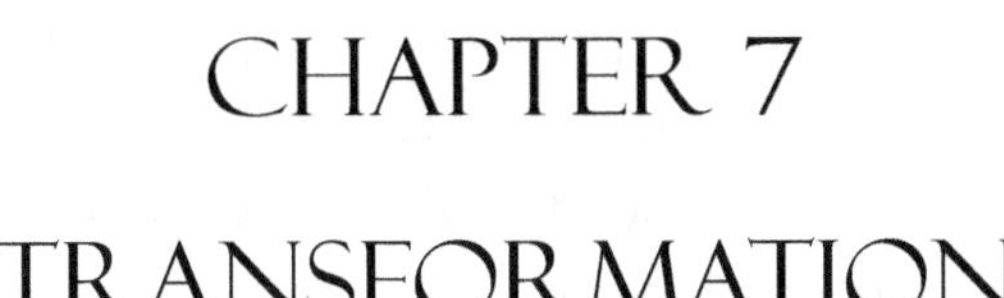

The thinning of the veil brings many challenges. It comes with confusion and resistance. I would often hear my critic during my inner work when I start to change. I had to heal the wounds and depend on faith to see me through. "We thank God for the word received through faith, not a human word but the word of God, which is indeed at work in you" (1 Thessalonians 2:13). "When we open up to hurt, it reveals our wholeness." (Harvey, 124) Our ego reacts to the threats and starts rumbling all kinds of noise. In the beginning, it was hard to hear my true self with all the chattering. I stuck with it and when I did the voice got smaller over time. I realize I was feeding my ego so long that it was not accepting the change so easy. It is a continuous growth process. It gets better! "For the body without the spirit is dead, and so is faith without works" (James 2:26).

When we hang in there that is when the break-through comes; life transformation. It was hard seeing other people enjoy outings and events while I stayed back to research or study! I thought *you would enjoy the fruit of your labor, keep going!* Through the transition, I encounter new relationships that had meaning and a fulfilling career. I remember when I had only one dollar, and that morning I pray for a cup of coffee. I also visualize what it would taste like if I could get it. I went to McDonald's that day, and to my surprise, the coffee was at a discount of twenty-seven cent for that week. I thank God. Gratitude helps me a lot to reach where I am today. I stop focusing on problems and find something that day to be grateful.

Self-mastery comes when we are aware of reality and the part we play in the universe. I start to evolve when I temporary separated myself from family and friends that did not want to change. I realize I would feel at peace after giving myself mind treatment; my friends would come and dump their gossip on me. I start to get headaches listening to it day after day. They would feel great after talking to me; leaving me empty. I thought, *did we interexchange energy?* I start to become aware of my environment. I put a complete stop to it! They must learn to do their inner work and stop being an energy vampire! I had to do my work for self-discovery, why should I feel sorry for them. I had to work on myself day after day, and it was painful. I wanted to transition into a new consciousness to help myself and others. "When you go through deep waters, I will be with you. When you go through rivers of difficulty, you will not drown. When you go through the fire, you will not burn; it will not consume you" (Isaiah 43:2).

I start to think about the law of gravity. It works well in the universe to correspond to our vibration or rhythm, "as above so below." Therefore, I concluded the law of the mind must work in the same way; "And so it is" (Masters, 29). Every day I had to be conscious of my thoughts. As it enters my mind, I would listen to it without judgment. Fighting against my thoughts bought more negative thinking. Thoughts are seeds planted in our higher consciousness and returned to us in the physical world. "Be not deceived, God is not mocked; for whatsoever a man soweth, that he shall reap" (Galatians 6:7-9).

"Nothing beautiful comes without some suffering" (Lama & Tutu, 43). For many years I had dreams and goals. "Hope deferred makes the heart sick, but dreams fulfilled is a tree of life" (Proverbs

13:12). I had to master myself and stop being lazy, sitting and hoping something would come my way. I start acting! I recall having a dream of someone handing me a stack of books. As I held it in my hand, the stack was higher than above my head. So, I ask the lady in the dream, *why so many books*?" She replied, "that is how much you need to catch up!" As I woke up from the dream, it pricked my heart. My life had no meaning at the time, and I had no goals set for myself. I would go home crying to God about the earth and never did anything to improve myself and the life of others. "You unbelieving and perverse generation, Jesus said, "how long shall I stay with you?" (Matthew 17:17).

I had another dream of me searching for something. It is, "Looking or finding part of self" (Inserra, 358). I use my dreams to guide me on my journey. As I recall another dream, my heart was on the Tv screen beating. "It is a positive sign of self-knowledge" (Inserra, 85). However, what scared me the most about my dreams was the tornado. When I first start to master myself, I had dreams of storms. Meaning; "transition major life change" (Inserra, 398). I start to notice my life was changing and my old belief system was being broken down. Source energy cannot be destroyed. I knew there is greater power and I realize the key to one's suffering is a part of life.

It helps us develop compassion. If Nelson Mandela did not spend twenty years in prison, *would he be part history today?* He develops who he was and why he came to earth. Realizing his enemies were human too who have fears and expectations. He received a Nobel prize after his suffering. I start to go with the flow of life and keep good thoughts about myself and others. We all are important because we all are working with one law; energy!

To master oneself, *how do we remain joyful in the face of adversity?* We must be honest with ourselves that it is painful but see the opposite polarity of it. "We have no control over our feelings, emotions are spontaneous that arise" (Lama & Tutu, 46). Even Buddha practice mind training in Tibetan. The teaching focus on the key point of, "lessening one's self-absorption" (Lama & Tutu, 48).

I stop focusing on my problems and came up with creative ideas to solve it. If I am unable to fix something, it is ok! I ask myself, *what am I learning from this?* Then I release it, and the answers often come to me later.

Later in life, I found out I had a divine partner who helped me on my journey. Most people call it twin flame. It was different from the soul mates I encountered. It was the shadow of myself. It hit trigger points in my life that I never knew existed. It was painful! I learned self-control from the encounter. I even release him back to God and had to grow within myself without feeling needy for him. I cried, kick, and had another pity party.

It was almost like I heard God say, "that is my divine love, now get to work!" I sure did, I completed three manuscripts and went back to studying metaphysic; reading all kinds of books and enter graduate school to obtain my master's degree in psychology. Without the shift into higher consciousness, I would still be sitting and hoping for change.

During the shift, I went through a stage of poverty. I told myself, keep creating, and the seed that you sow, so shall you reap! I prayed to God to return my divine partner, but I was being taught to release co-dependency, another false belief. I start to develop unconditional love for him and everyone! "Take delight in the Lord, and he will give you the desires of your heart" (Psalm 37:4). I notice when we discover ourselves, we find out about everyone else intentions in our life. I knew people were being used as a catalyst for me to wake up from the illusion I was living. When I would give up hope, I would see synchronicity; number sequence. I start to study it, to become aware of myself and the message from the universe.

I know it is a lifelong journey but living in the moment is all we have. I base my life on this truth. "The pain that you've been feeling is nothing compared to the joy that is coming" (Roman 8:18). As I was writing, this verse came to mind. I could not help but to search the meaning of 8:18. "Giving, receiving, life cycle, abundance, and faith with the universe." We know if we turn that eight sideways it is the mathematical number of *infinities*! The spiritual aspect of us there is no beginning or end. Energy can never be destroyed! "Jesus looked at them and said, with man this is impossible, but with God all things are possible!"

# CHAPTER 8

# HIGHER SELF

When I first start out to change the direction of my life, it came from hardship and a desire to learn. It causes me to go within. My persona was a tough outer shell, but I had to own up to my vulnerable part of myself. Becoming aware of it, allowed me to let go of control! As I start to research and reading, there were three stages to awaken to our true self. The first stage was self-discovery. "In this stage, we explore all aspect of ourselves. We shed off the life constriction of false belief, behavioral patterns, recognize our emotions, to become whole, and to fulfill our potential" (Harvey, xvi). The second stage is transformation. In this stage, we stabilize the changes we made in the first stage. We become passionate about ourselves and the world around us. We continue the journey of inner work. *How can we reach permanent changes?* We start to master ourselves in the process as we learn and grow. "In the third stage, is the source of higher consciousness. In this stage, we recognize reality and have transcendent." We know who we are and why we are here. We shed off the illusion and live in the present moment. "We live our divine nature by re-centering the true Self" (Harvey, xvi).

Inner work is the *art of listening.* I always had a deep longing for truth and getting to know the divine. As I explore my inner self, I had to let go of attachments and relationships. I had to separate my belief from everyone else. I notice when I would stay in the company of others, I start to think what they thought. I knew this truth but, *why did I accept the beliefs of others*?

I lost myself in the environment. I had to re-shape my truth, own it, and live up to it! I became attached to doing I forgot about my being. I ask myself, *what is my heart desire?*

I had to be patient with myself as I continue the journey within. "Let us not be weary in well doing; for in due season we shall reap, if we faint not" (Galatians 6:9). The way we respond to our inner work is vital for success or failure. How I respond to adversity and not trusting the process means I lack faith within. I had to realize I was not alone on my journey and my higher consciousness (God) is guiding me. "Show me your ways, Lord, teach me the path of truth, for you are God, and I hope in you all day" (Psalm 25:4-5). Walking a path on earth solo is lonely, but I had the desire to know the truth. I had to treat myself when I master one aspect of me. No one will congratulate us when we are walking in truth but ourselves. I start to be kind to myself, *saying; good job!* "Well done good and faithful servant! Since you have been faithful with a few things, Come and share your master's happiness" (Matthew 25:23).

# CHAPTER 9

# SELF-DISCOVERY

When I accept a job as a residential assistant in a homeless shelter, I realize the reward was good. The pay was minimal compared to what I usually make. However, I had an end destination in mind, and I was following my life path from an inner knowing. At the time I was on-call and did not have a permeant shift. When a spot did come available, I turn it down because I was in graduate school studying psychology and a full-time writer. I was single and praying to God about my twin flame who cross my path to shift me into higher consciousness. He was the catalyst, and I started writing short stories and became a songwriter. I did not know God gives us choices to choose our life partner. I still seek the Lord for wisdom. "If any of you lack wisdom, let them ask God who gives generously, and it will be given." (James 1:5)

This guy I was asking God about would wait two days before he replied to my text messages. Our emotions and how we feel could cloud over our judgment. I never knew about catalyst relationships. *Why did God allow me to go through emotional pain?* "He heals the brokenhearted and binds up their wounds." (Psalm 147:3) To master ourselves we must get our emotions in check, so we could see our situation clearly. I walked in the woods and saw a heart on the tree and even pass wedding chapels. *Does that mean God said yes? If so, why was God allowing me to wait?*

I continue to work at the homeless shelter, and as I looked up, there was a man's image that disturbed me. We both became friends while I was there, and he was a resident. As I listen to his story of his mom dying in his arms, and he was in two car accidents; he became homeless! Despite his situation, his words of healing and faith had me in *ah*! He had self-control reframing from sexual encounters until he met this woman recently. We both was sharing our horror stories. I would whine to him about the guy I was dating ignoring me, and he would tell me about his new girlfriend using words to beat down his spirit. *Why did we endure this kind of abuse*? Most woman and men of God understand humanity and will forgive. However, let us not be fooled! "Do not believe every spirit but test it to see if it is from God. Many false prophets have gone out into the world." (1 John 4:1)

As I was walking through the woods again, I moved closer to the heart that was on the tree. To my surprise, it had two lines that cross through it. I heard a small voice that said, completion! God had already fulfilled his purpose in my life with my twin flame.

The guy at the shelter was beginning to heal, and he became vibrant! He did not need crutches anymore, and he started back going to the gym. I continue to talk to him over the next six months while working there. I notice the discipline he had for himself. He was a martial art training/ boxer. He started back training people again. I did not know at the time we were developing a passion for each other, but everyone saw it! We both saw and heard the presence of God in each other, and it was a blessing. I start to question God about my character. *Why was I drawn to a man at my place of employment?* The man stated I was his boss and it was true because residential assistant could report and write them up. I never saw it that way I saw myself as a servant, and I treated everyone equally.

Within that time, my director asks me to take on a part-time position on the weekend. I decline again and told her I will cover it for a month and follow-up. Well, every weekend I couldn't wait to have a meaning conversation with this man who appears to be homeless but, I saw greatness. Not only was I self-mastering myself but he was too. We never met outside the job or conversated on the phone. Outside of work, I continue to do research and study to reach consciousness.

Six weeks later, him and I desire a hug for meeting such a kind person. The more I listen to his story of the car flipping over; he jumped out of the car. He said a blue bubble light surrounded him. He kneels on his kneeled and said, "God save me!" He was an ex-king pin drug dealer in Barry farms, Panama City, New York, and other states. His brokenness came from the death of his father, mother, and car accidents. He went in the ring to take it out on a two-hundred and fifty-pound punching bag. The results were seen in his upper shoulders, back, arms, and stomach. He was a small size guy with a height of five foot eleven inches. His muscle build was proportion to his body.

Self- mastery comes in the form of brokenness. We both stood in the hallway on the second floor before he went inside his dorm. When life is broken down inside oneself, we feel the divine and love for humanity. As we both reach for a hug, we were overtaken by a passionate kiss. *Yikes*! We both stepped back and was in shock it even happened. He headed towards his dorm, and I stomp my foot down the steps, and I was upset with myself. *Lord, why is this happening now*? I have self-control with other men, *why not with him?* It is not right as I murmured to myself. *My character, moral values, and integrity in danger*? I am at work, and these are the people I want to help and serve.

I saw improvement in this guy life. He was now working a job and plan to leave the shelter in a month. He has his degree in biochemistry engineering. We both was on the same path of learning, but I was still unsure why we cross paths. I was in the medicine closet helping another resident to obtain his medication from a lock box. He turned to me and said, *"not everyone here are bad people you know?"* "The guy you are having a conversation with is a kind gentleman." He looks up into my eyes with concern as if he was a father. He said, "Do not miss your boat." "You know some people miss their chance." He shook his head as he proceeds to walk away.

I could feel a pulsation of a heartbeat in the middle of my belly as my palms start to sweat. I walked towards my desk, and the guy who he spoke about was coming around the corner. He smiled at me as he entered the elevator. I felt love bubbling up inside of me. I stared at the computer. *Lord save me, let not my integrity fall*! People watch us day after day for weeks, and I did not know they reported me. I was text by my director to visit her office. I entered the building my heart started to pound. A peace surrounded me. I step into her office, and before she said a word, I said, "I know why I am here. *"Oh yeah why don't you tell me about it*?" She said.

"It is the talk about him and me conversating at the desk?" "What is it with him walking you to your car?" "He only walked me to my car twice one time he was getting a car charger," I replied. "Then why did he get in the car after the staff pulled off?" I thought, what is she saying? "He was in my car for a minute and left." "No, he was in your car for a little over a minute and it was three times!" *oh my goodness is she kidding me*? "Are you having a romantic relationship with him?" I did not know how to answer my accuser, so I replied, "I have never seen him outside of work." "We are not having sexual relations!" "there are some feeling involved." "I take full responsibility for what I am feeling beyond my control." "I understand that, *but are you having a romantic affair*?" Why is she answering me the same question? *Did I not give her enough information?* "I take full responsibility for myself." "Your days here are over." She replied. "Okay, I will accept that" "Now moving forward with you and him, you do not even know that man." "I thought to myself, and neither do you, but you sat down and told him your life story. *Why is she questioning my future with him anyway*? Is this not unprofessional on her behalf? "I understand and thank you," I replied. Self-mastery is living in truth no matter what the consequence. I walked out of the building and said to myself, *Lord what are you doing?*

Within that following week, I was invited out to dinner by the man. He paid for our meal. Our dinner conversation was endless and truthful. I realize the director did not give me termination papers. *Why was I fired?* "When it was clear we could not persuade them, we gave up and said, "The Lord will be done!" (Acts 21:14) One thing I know about my self-discovery is I am shy. However, I have a bold spirit of truth. I learn self-control that day. It was all part of my destiny in learning and growing. Self-mastery is when we own up to our actions and move on. Stand for the truth and walk your journey! "Therefore, we have an opportunity, let us do good to all people, especially to those who belong to the family of a believer." (Galatians 6:10)

Before being terminated, I saw a home on the market. The original price was a million dollars. Now the seller is motivated to sell dropping the asking price to $924,900. I search the web the following week, and it was an open house. *Yes*! I thought, only if I could get in there to see inside of the place before going to work. "I will give you every place where you set your foot, as I promised Moses." (Joshua 1:3)

I pulled up to the home. It was a six bedroom and six baths. There was a married couple looking at the home. They stared at me as I entered. I smiled at the realtor because with God all things are possible! When we go into new territory and stretch ourselves, you will shake like a leaf! I walk in the home anyway. It was the most beautiful high ceiling home I ever saw. I finished my tour when the lady wanted me to fill out paperwork to leave my contact information. *Oh no! I was still shaking.* I filled it out and smiled at her. *"I hope you could read my chicken scratch?"* I said. She smiled back and said, "I sure can!" she offered me water, and I envision her welcoming me to my new home. I accept the water and exit out the front door.

"Lord I did it!" *"I was afraid, but have I not stepped my foot upon the land?"* I turned around and smiled at the home. I prayed that if that home drop to $800,000 I will purchase it. One month later I check the website and the home drop the asking price to $899,999. *Yes*! I will wait until they drop that $99,999 and its *mine*! Wait that is a message from the universe. Meaning of all 9's: lightworkers of the world embrace who you are, and divine justice at work. *If I want that home, I must work for it*? Sometimes we may look like a fool to others when we do the impossible. Do it anyway!

Self-control is when one knows and admit they are afraid, but one could control their emotion! I did what I desire to do for the day. At the time I enter the homeless shelter to start my shift. The guy was at the front door. We both arrived at 3 pm. "How was your day I ask him?" "My day was great my new co-worker took me out for lunch." "Nice" I replied. "How was yours?" "I just viewed the inside of a million-dollar home." I giggled. He took off his shades and stared at me. *"Are you thinking about purchasing a mansion?"* "Yes, I am." I smiled. He leaned toward me and said, "God scares me sometimes." *"What do you mean?"* "I saw in a vision I am a multi-billionaire. I smiled at him and said, "me too!" We both laugh, and people would walk around us with angry faces not even knowing the conversation we had.

Our later discussion he would say, "you have talk shows to go to." "Oprah likes your book, we are traveling the world and reaching lives." At that moment I knew my inside thoughts was speaking to me on the outside! His father pastored a church and taught him as a little boy until he was 16years old when he passed away. The homeless man was a mighty warrior of God place in the shelter. No one figured it out but me. I am a lucky lady! Through our adversity of him being homeless and me being fired, we gain insights into self-mastery.

"Consider it all joy when we encounter various trials, knowing it is testing our faith which produces endurance. Therefore, endurance has its perfect results, so you may be complete and perfect, lacking nothing." (James 1:2-4) Self-mastery to reach higher consciousness comes through and only adversity to bring about change in one's life!

# CHAPTER 10

# SET BOUNDARIES

*How many times we let people and do things in our lives we know we shouldn't?* We hear the gut instinct saying, *no?* We ignore that part of ourselves all the time. Once we become aware, there are no more excuses. It's time to learn and move forward in our life. People see you improve your life and want to throw their problems on you! Don't sit there for hours talking about their bad times. Give them advice and send them on their way. You don't have to solve everyone problems! Make a concise decision to help them or not! Empath gets overwhelmed with people problems. It happened in my life trying to save people from bad choices. It's their responsibility. I had to fix my problems. I learned and grew from it. Let them learn and experience life.

I was having a conversation with someone, and he told another man how he saved money living in a homeless shelter. It made me sick to my stomach. *Why would someone want to live in the shelter to save money? What will they do with the money?* I even saw people going inside shelters to live and eat for free. "For even when we were with you, we gave you a rule: the one who is unwilling to work shall not eat." (2 Thessalonians 3:10) I am not speaking of those who need help from abuse, addictions, or been in a car accident. I saw people sitting around waiting on a disability check when they were capable of working. I saw all this while working for a homeless prevention shelter.

We are disappointed at society! There are people with disabilities who want to work in the community to have a quality of life, *but the people who are not disabled want to be.* Do not feel sorry for these people and set boundaries against them! Give them words of encouragement and speak to those dry bones. Do not give your money! Do not put them in your home! Do not give too much of your time! You have no idea of the problems that come with it. It will drain your energy and cut off your flow of wealth if you let it.

As an empath, I had to learn to stabilize my emotions. "If anyone will not welcome or receive your words, leave that place and shake the dust off your feet." (Matthew 10:14) I am glad I know this now! Let's speak about the millionaire and billionaire because I know people will be hit with their critic soon enough. Just because you are wealthy do not mean you should send your money where people tell you too. I will choose to serve the community with my heart and be joyful in my given. If not, my services were pointless to myself and humanity. "Each one must give as he has decided in his heart, not reluctantly or under compulsion, for God loves a cheerful giver." (2 Corinthians 9:6-7) Stop feeling like you should save everyone!

People should set boundaries against those who are always looking for free services and advice all day long! People are sitting around all day and expecting people to deliver them. Stop letting people overwhelm you. I see pastors and life coaches getting drained. Everything comes with a price and a cost of service and time. I had to invest in my life by attending seminars, paying editors, or business deals. We need to allow other people to do the same. They will start taking their lives more seriously. I remember when I was receiving financial aid at college. I didn't work as hard. I didn't become aware until I saw the thousands of dollars owed on my credit report. It became painful when I had to take $4,000 out of pocket to finish undergraduate classes to graduate. If we had to invest in ourselves its time for other people to step up and do it!

Another boundary I had to set is the relationship with friends. If they are always talking about going to a party, *how far will that take you in life*? The time and money wasted could have been invested. People say they don't have money to start a business, but if they add up all the money, they party with it's over a thousand dollars. When I use to party with a coworker, she would spend $100 a night on drinks and food for us. It was on Friday and Saturday. I did the math in my head while out partying and it made me sick to my stomach! I became aware of myself and other people bad habits. Two hundred dollars a week times 52 week (a year) is $10,400. These are the same people who sit around saying the rich people have privilege. They don't know what wealthy people had to give up living their dream life. The question is, *how bad do you want it*?

I don't see people wanting it bad at all. On social media, I post a lot of inspirational quotes and no one like it but my sister! Then other people post foul language and funny videos downgrading others, and it is a laugh or joke of the day! Many likes and laughter. I start to hurl in my stomach again! I had to separate myself from it and started groups with lightworkers and soul connections! We must get to a point in life where we are obsessed with success. I learn to wake up with it, eat with it, breath with it, and sleep with it! I start to evolve when I set boundaries!

People that became wealthy most went through adversity. I hear people talking about celebrities. Saying what they did not do for the poor people. *People are always looking to the rich people to solve problems. What have those complainers done for society*? Rich people were in lack just like you, they just made a conscious choice not to be anymore. I made a sacrifice. I did not shop for years. I only had red lobster once a year or not at all (which I love so much). I did not make it to the family function because I didn't have gas money to get there! I didn't ask people to keep saving me. As a single parent of four children which I only had three to provide for, I had to figure out how I was going to get out of this rut. I had no financial help from the fathers. "My suffering was good for me to be afflicted, that I might learn my statutes." (Psalm 119:71)

I started investing in my life and was willing to do whatever it takes. I spend money to attend classes instead of buying new shoes. People didn't know I had holes in the bottom of my shoes. I try my best to stand firm on the ground so that no one would see it. I was okay with it because my money was invested in things that was important to me. I spend $1,000 for an application to enter graduate school at George Washington University. It gave me joy when I got accepted because the school has the highest competitor who applies. Also, I spend $3,400 to self-publish my first book because they did not have payment plans, then money spent on my second, third books, and songwriting. *Could I smell and taste the red lobster I didn't have for the year*? If I get myself out of this, I knew I could have it every day if I wanted it! "I kept my body under subjection, lest that by any means when I preach to others, I should be cast away." (1 Corinthians 9:27)

Those who set up a lifestyle for themselves set the boundaries. Don't let people come and share when they did not put in the work. I am not speaking about family. Gather them up and teach them! Help them get their mind out the rut and others, not their finances. If you keep giving money, you will always give until their mind is healthy and healed. If they get their mind out, everything else will follow.

Regarding partners set boundaries. Believe whatever the person said reckless about themselves. Listen very carefully to the words people speak. The problem I had was I depended on my emotions and did not use logic. Set the tone of how you want to be treated and the things you will and will not accept. "Do not give dogs what is sacred: do not throw your pearls to pigs. If you do, they may trample them under their feet, and turn and tear you to pieces." (Matthew 7:6) *How many times after leaving a relationship we had to rebuild our self-worth*? It takes too much energy and time. Set the boundaries!

# CHAPTER 11

# HANDLING GRIEF

Grief does not only come from the death of a loved one. Grief is sadness, heartache, pain, affliction, and distress. All forms of grief place a burden on the physical body. I suffer many years of sorrow and pain. To master yourself the key is being aware it is happening to you. For years I was in the denial stage. *How will one reach the permeant changes of being their self*? They must go through a transition and know where they at in the process to be free. There are five stages of grief. The stages are denial, anger, bargaining, depression, and acceptance. There are many standpoints to view it. I am going to speak from a relationship perspective first.

In the first stage, we are in denial. *We know when we first meet someone, and they start to talk, they are not for us right*? We dismiss our intuition and would rather focus on the abdominal muscles, pretty hair, nice eyes, or the way they make us feel in bed. We know we should have run a long time ago. In the second stage, we are now angry because our partner ignores us, *but we not mad at ourselves for ignoring our intuition.* We angry because they cheated on us, but we are the ones who cheated ourselves by settling for less. The anger comes out in an uproar now we tell them to leave (which you don't mean). So, the next stage is bargaining. You plead for them to stay blaming yourself for the relationship problems, not knowing they just hit you with reverse psychology. *Guess who gets the treats*? They do because you take them out to dinner or cook a nice meal and have sex.

Then you wake up in the morning and still not happy with the choices you made. So now you are in the third stage, depression. You can't move out of bed; you were up all night worried where were they *until 5 am in the morning*? You let this person take away your sleep, your peace, and your joy. If you have children, *what's going on with them*? Now the kids out of control in the home and school. *Do they deserve to be yelled at*? You have no idea they feel your energy now everyone in the house is suffering. *Do you want to know what's going on in your inside world? Look at your children are they calm or out of control*?

If you don't handle this and get it under control within yourself (the outside forces will follow) you will go through what I went through, attempted suicide! The last stage is acceptance. We realize the problem and face it. Some people handle it differently. While others will let go of the bad relationship and move on as they accept it, they are some who will stay together and deal with what the person is doing to them and live the rest of their life miserable. Be aware of these stages and pull your mind out of it. I am not a physician so if you seek medical attention go to the doctor and get medicine for your depression if you choose to. It's your conscious choice. As a healer, I am teaching you to get to the root of the problem.

Handling grief from a death is still the same approach. The denial stage is when we are not crying saying we are okay. It's good to release the emotion so it won't block the flow of energy within. Sitting around in the room acting like it didn't happen is denial. Next, your anger started to boil within you and now you mad at God. It was my experience sitting around wasting my life because I didn't want to move on. I was angry because I felt like if God took him, *why doesn't he just take me too*? Then I start to bargain with the Lord and say if only you have him stay; I would have been better off. When God ignore our barging, we hit the depression stage. We lost, afraid, and can't see hope. It was a time for me to think to always forgive others and never take anyone for granted. The last stage in acceptance, it's when we learn, grow, and evolve. Death does not have a date on it like the birth certificate. We must make meaning of a good life while on earth. When famous people died, they left behind a legacy. We should strive for the best version of ourselves. I don't want my children to weep all day for months. Let them cry and say my mom touch many lives. It will inspire them to finish what I started, but they will be greater than I am because we all evolve and grow.

Those who encountered a twin flame relationship (including myself). We go through different stages to reach transformation. We feel the bliss of love. We feel it because we are love. *Then you go through separation feeling your heart rip out of your chest and can't explain what happened*? The stages are grieving because the pain of separation, disbelief that you came across this great love, hatred towards the person because you believe they took your heart, but what they snatched was your ego. Next forgiveness as you continue to emerge into oneness with yourself and God as you accept what is happening. Final stage is surrender to God will for your life. Never ignore or run. I ran for seven years. I kept saying I am not ready for my twin flame. What I didn't know it was showing me I am not going to accept myself. I was stuck in the pain stage for years. Oh, boy, did I suffer.

# CHAPTER 12

# GRATITUDE

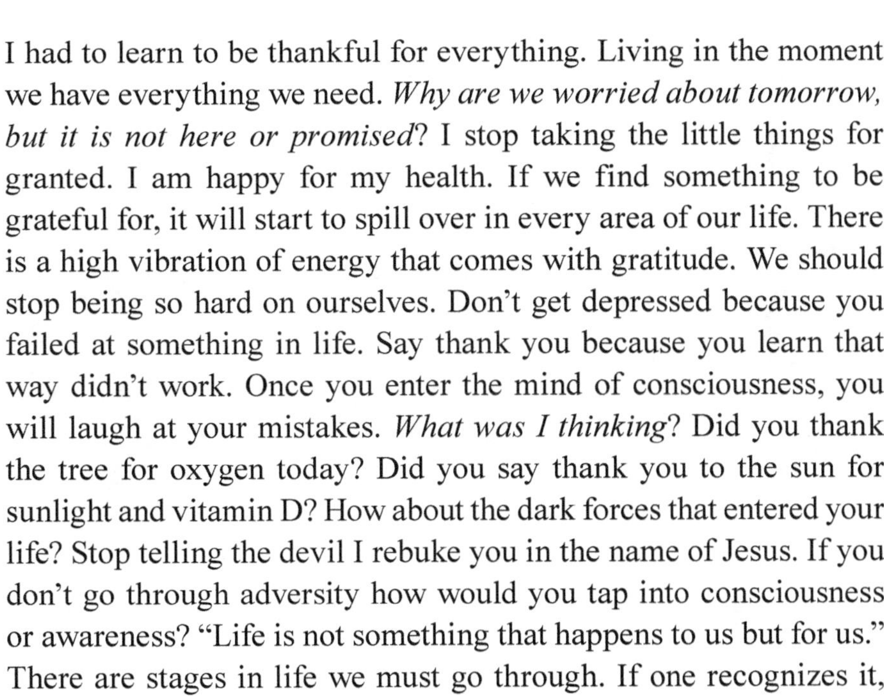

I had to learn to be thankful for everything. Living in the moment we have everything we need. *Why are we worried about tomorrow, but it is not here or promised*? I stop taking the little things for granted. I am happy for my health. If we find something to be grateful for, it will start to spill over in every area of our life. There is a high vibration of energy that comes with gratitude. We should stop being so hard on ourselves. Don't get depressed because you failed at something in life. Say thank you because you learn that way didn't work. Once you enter the mind of consciousness, you will laugh at your mistakes. *What was I thinking*? Did you thank the tree for oxygen today? Did you say thank you to the sun for sunlight and vitamin D? How about the dark forces that entered your life? Stop telling the devil I rebuke you in the name of Jesus. If you don't go through adversity how would you tap into consciousness or awareness? "Life is not something that happens to us but for us." There are stages in life we must go through. If one recognizes it, they will face it. Most people go through pain and want to argue or fight against it. "Submit yourself to God, resist the devil and he will flee from you." (James 4:7) I am not going to spend my time and energy fighting the devil or dark forces. They help me in the process of evolution, *thank you!*

# CHAPTER 13

# REPEATING NUMBERS

*Why did God give us the ability to visualize and the mind to think?* It is our only way out from unconsciously moving off autopilot. We should always operate from the consciousness. The mind expands and is very creative. The universe sends us messages in images and numbers. God gives us the vision to formulate the formula for our life. When we think from the image we want and not the situation (outside circumstances) our mind will come up with a solution.

A lot of people are seeing numbers in the form of 11,22,33,44,55,66,77,88,99 or zeros. People do not take the time out to decipher the meaning. It was a wake-up call for me. There are unseen forces helping us. "When the student is ready the teacher will appear." Sometimes we get frustrated with our slow growth of process to only look up at the clock, tags on cars, billboard, and see the universe speaking to us. You can call it God if you like. Its all source energy. When you leave your physical body, it is a lighter version energy field of yourself. We had to come in a physical body in the third dimension because that is the only way we could see each other. On the other hand, spirit realms don't have dense bodies, neither do God. *Have you seen God?* Therefore, communication is in the intuition (energy), images, and numbers. Based on what we are going through at the time we must decode it.

We all start seeing 11:11 first. This number shown is manifestation is taking on its form. Pay attention to your words and thoughts because it's all energy. If you are thinking about entering a relationship and you see these numbers 222 don't be afraid to do so. The 2's are partnership or business partner. The numbers appearing in the form of 333 are ascended masters, it could be deciphered in two ways. One, you have transcended and are the expert of your life and are qualified to coach others. If you did not cross the threshold, then there are ascended experts coming to teach you. The form of numbers appearing 44 are angels. These are your angel guides. Do not be afraid to ask for help. They will not intervene in your life unless you ask them. Everyone is assigned to an angel or archangel.

Changes come in the form of 55. It is either from the transformation, poverty to success or single to married. When seeing 66 don't be afraid because a lot of people say it is the mark of the beast. However, 66 is the material world. Our thoughts do not always have to focus on material possession. It should be balanced with spiritual and material. In the image of 77 is miracles. Get ready to receive it. It is your blessing from the life you created in your mind, acted, and now miracles are showing up everywhere. The numbers of 88 are abundance. It comes in all forms. It could be good or bad depending on the thought you held.

*How many times you hear wealthy people speak good about money, and money keep showing up? In contrast how many complainers get more of what they are complaining about?* Self-mastery is using everything for your good and not against you. The final number image of 0's is you are doing great work! Take these numbers and decipher what is going on in your life and decode it. You can also do your research. Whatever resonates with you don't ignore the message if you want to reach higher consciousness.

# CHAPTER 14

# RESULTS

Before I get into the deep thinking in the way I believe life works, I am going to use the analogy of video games. My favorite game when I was a kid was Mario. I would beat all these lifeforms in the game to only get closer to fighting the dragon. The little things before him was simple. For instance, stopping on the turtle head to get me a mushroom to eat or coins. No matter what we fought in the game it was either prizes or coins. When I became a teenager, I stop playing video games. *Did I know I was playing the game of life*?

People think they got their life all figured out. *Are we fooling ourselves*? Don't hide behind the degrees as I did. Start mastering yourself. People are proudful of a good credit score, but they are working for someone else to maintain it. Don't confuse movement with progress. Just because you are on the go in life (the grind) don't mean you are getting things done. You go to work, pay bills, watch Tv, eat, bathe, sleep, and maybe parties here and there. *When you wake up in the morning, do you repeat the cycle? Are you proud of yourself*? We can train a robot to do that. In fact, there are robots in different countries taking over. Bank tellers only have a select few tellers because of technical ability to deposit checks from the mobile phone.

When I heard about telemedicine in college, I knew I had to change my life fast and evolve or get left behind. The world is shifting to another dimension, and if people don't wake up off autopilot, they will work for these robots. Then they will continue to complain that the robots forgot to pay them. *Let's see you keep that credit score up now.* Let's start taking control over our destiny.

A lot of people do not want to leave the old paradigm behind to enter the unknown. We all need to enter consciousness so that we can evolve, we been stuck here too long. The paradigm is a mental program system. When babies come into the world, they see through the eyes of consciousness. I would never forget when my mom was in the hospital and my little sister was born. She lifted her head to look into my mom's eyes. Doctors say babies can't hold their head up or focus the eyes when coming into the world. She did that day! *Was she trying to tell my mom something?* Did the children forget why they here and adapt to the old paradigm structure or belief? *When we find ourselves, we return to this source energy?*

I attend Bob Proctor seminar, and I am blessed beyond measures! He spoke about understanding *the magic of life.* First, we must understand everything is energy and we are in the form of God (made in his image). Bob Proctor spoke of three concepts: thoughts are spiritual (God mind), ideas are intellect, and things are physical. We must learn to work the body, mind, and spirit as one unit. I learn this concept in metaphysical from Dr. Master's class. Bob Proctor spoke about the conscious and subconscious mind. It is a starting point and is very helpful. I learn in metaphysical teaching there are many levels within a human mind. 1). conscious 2). subconscious 3). Psychic exchange 4). unconscious. 5). pure mind(consciousness).

People that went unconscious or in a coma comes back with stories of understanding something clearly about the light or dark forces. Some people get to the point where they can hear other people's thoughts or sense energy. We all have the ability. "Then God called out, Samuel! Samuel said yes, I'm here. He ran to Eli and said, did you call me? Eli said I did not call you. Samuel heard the voice the second and third time. He said yes, you did call me. Eli said go back to bed and if the voice appears again, say speak Lord your servant hears." (1 Samuel 3:4-10) It happened in my life when I got distracted from my five senses. I learn to listen to the Lord with my heart(intuition) or gut feeling.

According to Dr. Master's class and Bob Proctor theory, they both have similar approaches to life forces.

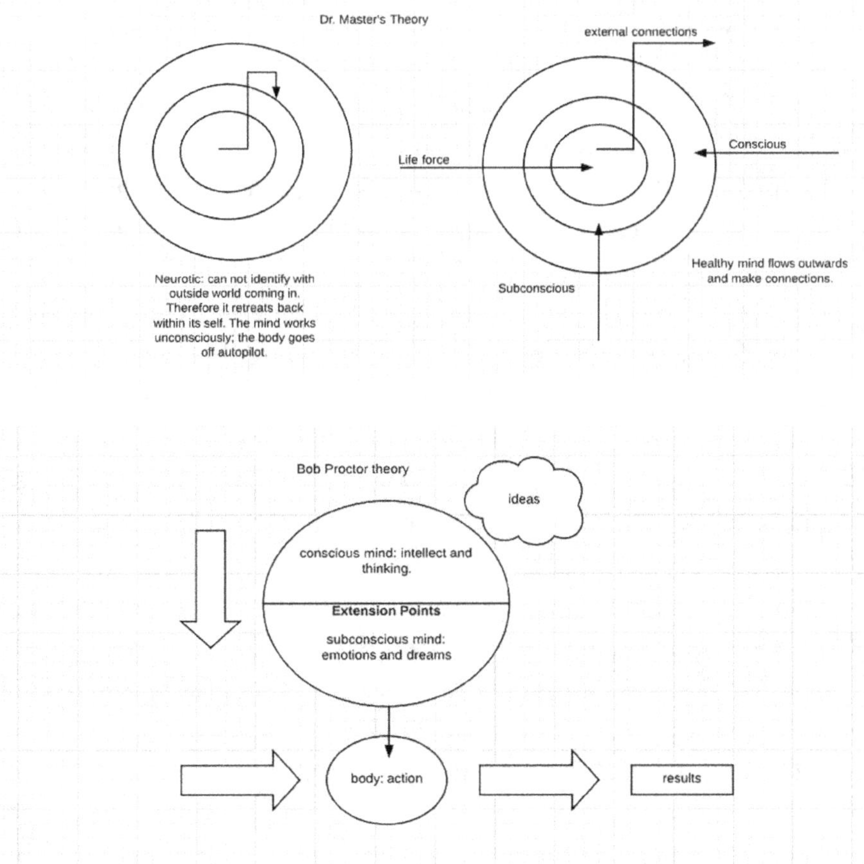

Take the thoughts and ideas and move it to the subconscious mind getting the emotions involved. When they all work together, it is oneness. Your mind of creativity inside move into the external world. Never allow the environment program your subconscious mind. The body will still react bringing unwanted results.

Dr. Master used the term traditional mindset. He stated the person could not connect to the outside world coming in. Therefore, they create an illusion in their subconscious mind to escape their reality. The term neurosis is a mental illness. It is manipulation, antisocial behavior, and mind playing games. Psychotherapy helps in this process, bringing one back to the identity of oneself. Their subconscious mind must be reprogrammed.

Our feedback from our life is the environment around us. If you don't like the world, you created to change the "paradigm". Bob Proctor spoke about working from the inside out in the diagram. In this process the change manifest fast. Before I enter his online training, those forces were manifesting in my life. I did not know how, but his diagram explained it.

Chemistry speaks about molecules as it changes its environment. In our body the energy field aura radiant with colors and vibration depending on negative or positive thoughts. These are the forces that go forth in the universe and get sent back into our lives. *Why did the school system tell us to live by our five senses*? Therefore, the school system is failing. Never live by what you see. Create the image and bring forth fruit in your life.

Bob Proctor said there are three income strategies. One percent of the population create multiple streams of income. Three percent invest money to make money. Ninety- six percent exchange their time for money. They are punching the clock to work for others. I start to feel sick when I heard this. "Money is a faithful servant," and should always work for us. The cause of good fortune is aware in the shift of paradigm. Shift it and let it work from inner to outer and your life will change forever. Ninety-six percent of the world do not operate like this.

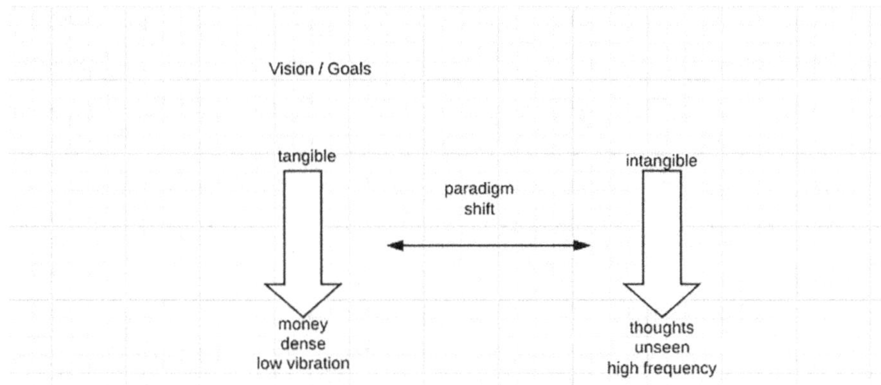


Never fight against your current circumstance. The thoughts of money came from someone mind to create it. *So why are people waiting for money to make the dream a reality?* They should move their vibration to a higher frequency. Therefore, think the thought of how to get the money to complete the goal instead of waiting for the money to come; you will be waiting forever!

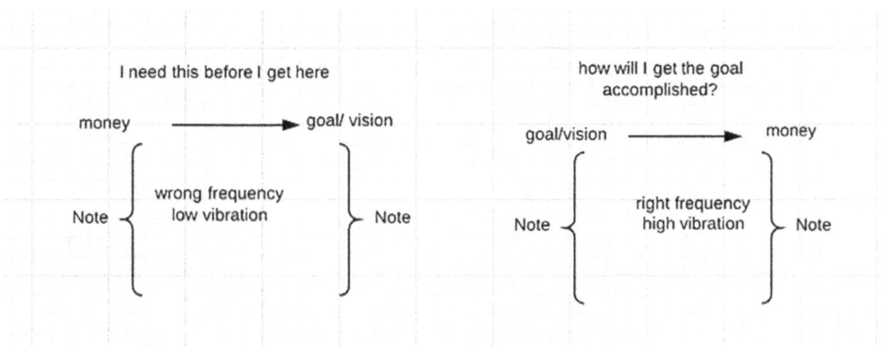


The mind will come up with creative ideas because it is on the highest form of vibration. Do what you see in the next step of the process. *Is it a credit card? Borrow money from a friend?* Do whatever it takes! My example, I wrote all my books first. I start creating from a high vibration of thoughts. *How did I get the money?* I use my income tax return. *How many of us take that money and go shopping?* I did that for years! When that was done, I utilize my graduate loans. Operating in a higher frequency nothing is scary or impossible! I knew people who took business loans to start their business. They paid it back and had streams of income coming in. It is a lot of grant money out there for business waiting to be created. We need to research for it. If it is something you are passionate about, you will find a way. My mom always told me, "if there is a will there is a way."

Bob Proctor explained the law of compensation. *Is there a need for what you do? Do you have the ability to do it? How difficult is it to replace you?* You must believe in your heart you are here on a mission and no one can fulfill that dream in your heart but you. Obsession is the key to open the heart and move towards consciousness!

# CHAPTER 15

# SUPERNATURAL

Living a balanced life is having a prosperous soul. "Beloved I wish above all things that you prosper and be in good health, even as your soul prospers." (3 John 2) It is emotionally whole. The problem is not the spirit. It is the soul, the transformation of the mind. We must learn to master ourselves. Paul spoke about self in the Bible. "For the good that I want to do, I do not; but the evil I do not want to do, that I practice." (Romans 7:19) *Have you ever had a mental battle?* Once the soul prospers, it is the gateway for the supernatural. "I press towards the mark for the prize of the higher calling of God in Christ Jesus." "Let us be perfect be thus minded." (Philippians 3:14-15)

Everything we need in life we already have it. We have love, wealth, and health. It is manifested by a prosperous soul. "God has not given us a spirit of fear or timidity, but of power, love, and discipline." (2 Timothy 1:7) "No good thing will he withhold from them." (Psalm 84:11) Transformation is a process. "Do not despise the days of small beginning for the Lord rejoice to see the plumb line in Zerubbabel's hand." (Zechariah 4:10) *Do you think you found God?* "You did not choose me, but I chose you and appointed you so that you might go and bear fruit. Fruit that will last and whatever you ask in my name the father will give you." (John 15:16)

We have the responsibility to transform our thinking. It is not the devil. You are destroying yourself! "But each person is tempted when they are dragged away by their evil desire and enticed." (James 1:14) Our destiny is determined by the choices we make. "He must increase, and I must decrease." (John 3:30) It is allowing the consciousness to come through to the conscious mind. The flesh is crucified and living through higher self.

Thoughts are the lifeline. We must mentally prepare ourselves for where we are going and not the current state of being. "Have I not commanded you? Be strong and courageous. Do not be afraid. Do not be discouraged. For the Lord, your God will be with you wherever you go." (Joshua 1:9) Supernatural comes forth believing all that was promised to you! "Call those things which be not as though they were." (Romans 4:17) When we start thinking like God our life transform into the divine plan. It is the supernatural. The present state of being is walking in revelation. Faith is counted as righteousness! It is what brings the things God has provided for us from the spiritual realm into the physical. (Hebrew 11:1) From another perspective, it is the law of the universe. We vibrate in our body according to what we believe.

There is always a brick wall that blocks the promise land. "On the seventh day, Israelites got up and march around the town. This time they went around seven times." (Joshua 6:15) There must be a plan of action to move towards the supernatural. Afterward, stop and be patience. "Therefore, put on the full armor of God so that the day of evil(adversity) comes you may be able to stand your ground, and after you done everything, stand!" (Ephesians 6:13) It is a ripple effect that manifests beyond our imagination. "When the trumpet sounded the army shouted the wall collapsed; so, everyone went straight in and took the city. (Joshua 6:20) You do not have to understand it because you are thinking in the natural. Stand on the word and believe and see the supernatural! Plant the seed and be unshakeable. *"Do you believe that I am the father and the father is me?"* The words I say to you I do not speak on my own authority. Rather, it is the father living in me, who is doing his work.

Everything that you birth in the flesh that is bringing you heartache and pain, God said to cast out the bondwoman. "For my thoughts are not your thoughts, neither are your ways my ways, declares the Lord." (Isaiah 55:8-9) I prayed and asked that you be transformed to reach higher consciousness that you may be complete and whole lacking nothing! Then you will hear a voice that says, "Well done good and faithful servant!" (Matthew 25:21)

For years I kept telling my family I am going to make 1.4 million. My oldest brother challenge that thought by saying, *"where it is?" "I don't see it yet!"* Back then that's all it was just a thought. I had no plan of action. I didn't even know where to start. I went to a couple of open houses. I knew the home I wanted. I already saw myself driving my dream car. I saw the contribution I wanted to make in the world. As Napoleon Hill said, "think and grow rich!" My thoughts were already sending me in the direction of a prosperous soul. The seed was planted in my subconscious mind. All I had to do was *"reverse engineer"* to bring it into my reality. Having a definite purpose already set the margin to act out the life. It is not that people do not have what they want in life, it is the habit that they develop. The purpose is the end goal. *What do I need to do or focus on to get there?* The biggest mistake is focusing on the money. *What is the daily task that will move you towards the direction? Do you need to advance your skills, read a book, or do marking?* The different from rich and poor is one group think long term. They write out a five-year plan, break it down to one year, monthly, then daily. *How many people follow through?*

Think regarding services to others and not your own desperate needs. Poor and middle class buy liability. They spend it on their home and cars. However, wealthy people buy assets first. They invest in real estate or building apartment buildings etc. Rich people use their time wisely. Poor people sell their time for money. Wise people utilize their time, talents, and investments. "Wisdom is the principle of things, and with all thy getting get understanding." (Proverbs 4:5-9)

After improving your earning such as return on investments, its time to enjoy the fruit of your labor. For example, if someone wrote a song and received 50,000 because of the number one hit song, *why would they spend all the money up and become poor again*? Pay yourself first a ten percent and save it! Then the rest invest in something that you believe. In my life, I make sure it is a passion. *Is it cancer research? Building homes for the poor*? The money will multiple based on the energy you put into giving valuable services. It will bring you joy and fulfillment. *Can you feel how high you are vibrating now*? It's supernatural! Before you know it, it is multiple streams of income flowing through cash flow.

When I start publishing my books, I did not check with the publication to see how many books was being sold. I focus on my next project and the one after that. *In my heart, I wondered how many people life I help transformed*? It keeps me humble to know I am a co-creator. When the attention is focused on abundance and not adversity wealth comes flowing so fast and you become a magnet! The wealthy get wealth because that is what they focus on; multiplying. The poor continue to be poor because of their complaining and habits. A prospers soul brings forth a blessed life!

# BIBLIOGRAPHY

n.d

The Bible, King James Bible Version. Bible Gateway.
Retrieved from http://biblegateway.com

n.d

The Bible, New International Version. Bible Gateway.
Retrieved from http://biblegateway.com

Byrne, Rhonda 2006
*The Secret.:* Beyond Words Publishing.

Harvey, Richard 2013
*Your Essential Self.* Woodbury, MN: Llewellyn Publication

Inserra, Rose 2002
*Dictionary of Dreams.* Heatherton, Australia: Hinkler Books.

Kendall, R.T 2002
*Total Forgiveness.* Lake Mary, Florida: Charisma.

Lama, Dalai 2016
*The Book of Joy.* New York: Penguin Random House.

Masters, Paul Leon 1989
    Bachelor's Degree Level Lesson: Volume 1-4

Munroe, Myles 2001
    *Understanding the Purpose and Power of and Woman.* New Kensington, PA: Whitaker House.

Munroe, Myles 2017
    How to become a leader and break away from your struggling mind set. Retrieved from https://youtu.be/1FMUysy5fss

Proctor, Bob 2018 The Science of getting rich event online video

Tiberio, Stacey & Montpetit, Mignon 2016
    Probing Resilience: Daily Environment Mastery, Self Esteem, and Stress Appraisal: Volume *83*

Tutu, Desmond 2016
    *The Book of Joy.* New York: Penguin Random House.

www.ingramcontent.com/pod-product-compliance
Lightning Source LLC
Chambersburg PA
CBHW051719050726
47598CB00003B/970